The World of Dreams

The World of Dreams

By HENRI BERGSON

PHILOSOPHICAL LIBRARY

New York

Translated from the French by
WADE BASKIN

Printed in the United States of America

ISBN 0-8065-3091-X

The World of Dreams

INTRODUCTION

In the modern world there is an increasing
tendency to see the essence of reality and the
secret of the universe, not in the inertia of
matter, but in the movement of life. For the
particular orientation of contemporary thought
we are to a certain extent indebted to one man
who, unwilling to submit to a materialistic doc-
trine, took up the concept of vitalism forged
earlier by Schopenhauer and by virtue of the
eloquence of his expression, the clarity of his
thought, and the force of his sincerity, made a
lasting impression on a sceptical age.

The major works of Henri Bergson (1859-
1941) are probably more familiar to the general

public than are those of any other philosopher
of our century. The same holds true for some of
his minor works, one exception being the present
work on dreams, first given as a lecture before
the Institut Psychologique on March 26, 1901
and later published in the *Revue Scientifique*
of June 8, 1901. And one is tempted to attribute
the neglect in this instance to the nature of the
subject rather than to a lack of merit in the
work. Too many investigators seem unfortu-
nately to look with disdain or bias on the study
of the interpretation of dreams. Each culture
has or has had its interpreters, yet the scientific
literature on the subject suggests that, apart from
the contributions of groups associated with
Sigmund Freud, Alfred Adler, and C. G. Jung,
there has been little progress since Bergson at
the end of his enlightening study left us "at the
threshold of the mystery."

That repressed wishes seek expression in
dreams was a common belief among the ancients.
Xerxes was urged repeatedly in his dreams to
undertake the invasion of Greece. He renounced
the idea only after he was told by Artabanus
that his dreams were nothing more than the
expression of thoughts that had been on his mind

during the day. Lucretius subsequently observed that whatever our hearts are set upon will be the subject of our dreams; he was supported by Cicero, who added that dreams are influenced by the overflow from our waking life, and by Plotinus, who noted that in dreams phantasy presents us with the object of our desire.

Another common belief among the ancients was that some dreams warn the sleeper that sickness or disease is imminent. Aristotle explained this; he pointed out that the sleeper has the ability to convert slight sensations into intense ones; he observed, for example, that a sleeper may dream of walking through fire when he perceives a slight sensation of heat on some part of his body. But the ancients insisted that while such dreams may be caused by immediate circumstances, others are unquestionably of divine origin.

They supposed that in sleep we sometimes have direct visions of the future or receive symbolic visions that can be interpreted by the expert. People possessed of the ability to interpret dreams have generally been held in high esteem by their associates. The Bible tells us that Joseph was made ruler over Egypt as a result of his proven skill in interpreting dreams. The

Greeks relied heavily on their interpreters. It was the practice of the Greeks to go to the temple of Aesculapius or to the temple of Apollo, perform or be subjected to certain rites and ceremonies, work themselves up into a state of exaltation, and fall asleep on the skin of a lamb that had been sacrificed. Afterwards they consulted the experts who explained to them the actual or symbolic meaning of their dreams. Aristotle even anticipated modern psychoanalytical thought by pointing out the element of distortion in dreams.

Bergson, who was acquainted with a vast body of Greek and Latin literature, succeeded in incorporating the best of contemporary thinking in all of his works. In his study of dreams, as in his other works, he gives ample evidence of his far-reaching scholarship, yet without ever appearing to flaunt it. Though his predilection for the well-chosen analogy may have carried him back to Plotinus, his tireless quest for truth made him range widely through books and periodicals written in English, French, and German.

In discussing different techniques for studying dreams, Bergson referred to the writings of D'Hervey and Ladd. In his analysis of the process of perception he cited the contributions of Goldscheider, Müller, and Münsterberg. His own ideas on the interpretation of dreams were drawn largely from the writings of A. Krauss. Finally, in dealing with the influence of incidental or repressed experiences on dreams, he alluded to Delage, Freud, and W. Robert.

Schopenhauer, (in *Parerga und Paralipomena*, Berlin, 1857) saw life as a ceaseless struggle against sleep and observed that when the intellect tires and demands sleep, the sleep that comes harbors for even the wisest man strange, senseless dreams. Like Schopenhauer, Tissié (in *Les rêves, physiologie et pathologie*, Paris, 1898.) held that the excitation of dreams may proceed from the sympathetic nervous system—that is, that derangements of the internal organs may provoke dreams or that dreams may reflect incipient changes in the condition of the body. Tissié also cited the case of a sleeper who when exposed to a bright light had a dream in which fire played an important part. Though psychoanalysts might stress a different aspect of the dream—the symbolic significance of such images as fire, water, chains, posts, and buildings—Bergson emphasized the fact that it was built around a visual sensation. Scherner (in *Das Leben des Traumes*, Berlin, 1861) was the first modern scholar to stress the importance of symbolism in dreams; he also saw in dreams a decentralization of the movement of life. Schopenhauer had phrased the same thought differently; he held that even when the intellect tires and suspends its functioning, the will continues to function.

Bergson in his discussion of the origin of dream-images (*souvenirs*, translated here as remembrances) relied heavily on an article written by Krauss (in *Allgemeine Zeitschrift für Psychologie*, XV and XVI, 1858-1859). In his article Krauss explained the origin of dream-images in this way: any sensation that is perceived during sleep awakens or evokes in the unconscious a related idea or image.

Delage (in *Revue Scientifique*, II, July, 1891) posited repressed materials as the main source of dreams. His article was of course published before Freud had announced his views on the subject. Bergson's lecture was delivered one year after the publication of Freud's epochal *Interpretation of Dreams* but long before Freud's theories had become a controversial issue. In his lecture and in a later statement, Bergson, who held that no part of our cumulative experience is ever lost, insisted that his views on the expression of repressed (not consciously formulated) wishes or fears are compatible with those of Freud.

Bergson's study of dreams, like all of his minor works, contributes an important share of his overall philosophy. He held that no universal system is valid; he nevertheless attacked a particular problem in each of his works and thereby elucidated a general philosophy of duration and movement.

Before his time most philosophers had attempted to define everything in terms of being, permanence, substance. Bergson started from the opposite point of view. He started from the assumption that the ultimate reality is time itself. In 1888 he finished the first of his major works, *Time and Free Will*. In 1896 he published the results of his study of memory, the means through which our existence is made continuous. *Matter and Memory* was followed in 1907 by the first philosophical masterpiece of our century, *Creative Evolution*. Midway between the last two works came his study of dreams, which has more than a chronological relation to both.

Bergson called dreams the direct link between sensation and memory. His studies of duration and movement had provided him with a broad base for his theory. With characteristic moderation and insight, he surmised that while our dreams are constructed around what we have seen, said, desired or done, their elaboration depends on memory-images collected and preserved since earliest childhood in "the innermost depths of the unconscious."

Only psychoanalysts have made a concerted attempt to penetrate the mystery surrounding the interpretation of dreams. Bergson's discussion of the dream in which fire played an important part was referred to earlier. Other typical dreams discussed in his lecture merit some comment in the light of psychoanalytical theory. As early as 1897, Mourly Vold had suggested, at the Third International Congress of Psychologists (Munich), that wish fulfillment, not posture, is responsible for dreams of flying. Freud saw in such dreams (when the whole body is not a phallic symbol) a desire on the part of the sleeper to relive childhood experiences. Freud also provided a psychoanalytical interpretation of the common dream of nakedness accompanied by embarrassment on the part of the dreamer but no sign of embarrassment on the part of observers. Contending that only those dreams in which the subject feels embarrassment deserve serious consideration, Freud attributed the vision of nakedness to a longing for a return to the days of pristine childhood when nakedness seldom occasioned expressions of ridicule or censure.

Experiments in progress at the University of Chicago since 1953 support Bergson's belief that dreaming is a normal process common to all and a vital link between perception and memory. Nathaniel Kleitman and William Dement in their investigations made use of a new discovery and an ingenious technique for determining with remarkable accuracy the exact moment when dreaming occurs. The information which they gathered from more than a thousand hours of sleep, though it uproots some popular beliefs on the subject of dreams, tends on the whole to reaffirm Bergson's statements.

Kleitman and Dement discovered that we tend to follow with our eyes the actions presented in our dreams. They were able by using electrodes and recording devices to chart the eye move-

ments and physiological reactions of their
subjects all during the night. On being awakened
at various stages during their dreams, the subjects
recorded their impressions while the dreams were
still fresh in their memories (or reported that
they had not been dreaming) and went back to
sleep.

Much was learned in these experiments about
the length and frequency of dreams as well as
about the subjects' reactions to them. We dream
on the average slightly more than one-fifth of the
time while we are asleep. Dreaming occurs sev-
eral times during the night but during only one
stage of sleep. We see spots, flashing lights,
blurred images as we drift to the brink of sleep.
Suddenly we plunge into a deep, apparently
dreamless sleep; dreaming that we can recall does
not occur until an hour or so later, after we have
gradually risen to the lightest stage of sleep; we
dream only about ten minutes during the light
stage in the first cycle; in succeeding cycles
sleep becomes progressively lighter and the
dreaming stage longer. As we approach the
dreaming stage in each cycle we become rest-
less; we roll and toss on the bed, adjust our arms
and legs, assume a new posture in anticipation of

the drama that is about to begin. Once the curtain goes up, we remain motionless until the end of the performance. We may repress some dreams on awakening, not so much because they are immoral or unpleasant, but because they occur at a low level of our mental activity—or as Bergson might phrase it, because we are then completely relaxed.

Two dreams recorded by Kleitman and Dement lend support to Bergson's conception of the constant interplay between perception and memory. The first illustrates our ability to incorporate in our dreams the data supplied by the senses while we are asleep, the second our ability to reproduce in our dreams images unconsciously perceived while we are awake. One subject was sprayed with water while a dream was presumably in progress and allowed to remain asleep for approximately thirty seconds. He reported on being awakened that he had been participating in a play when suddenly the leading lady fell. On rushing over to assist her, he felt water dripping down on his head. When he looked up, he saw that there was a hole in the roof. He dragged the lady off stage and rang down the curtain. A second subject looked on as a picture was flashed repeatedly on a screen, yet was unable to describe what he had seen. That night he dreamed, among other things, of a dog with silvery eyes and of a soldier with bulging eyes and a hideous grin. On being shown three different pictures after he awoke, the subject was able to select the one that had previously been flashed on the screen in front of him—a big automobile with an impressive grill.

Kleitman and Dement did not attempt to interpret the dreams recorded by their subjects. Deep sleep, according to Bergson, carries us far back into the past and provides a most fruitful field for psychic research. The evidence assembled by these two investigators, though it fails to yield any direct proof of the occurrence of dreams during deep sleep, does not actually contradict Bergson on this point. In some instances subjects whose eye movements had not been charted reported that they had been dreaming; in a few other instances subjects whose eye movements had not been charted reported that they had been dreaming. The exceptional cases raise the possibility that some dreams are actually accompanied by eye movements but not subject to recall while others are so remote from our consciousness as to entail no eye movement and be forever beyond recall.

In another lecture Bergson likened the functioning of our sensory organs to the intellect. Just as our intellect admits into consciousness only those memory-images that have a direct bearing on the present, so the sensory organs channel into consciousness only perceptions that are of some pragmatic worth. And just as the memory-images evoked by perceptions received through the senses are fringed by other vague images, so our perceptions may in turn be fringed by other vague (extra-sensory) perceptions. Bergson observed in his lecture on dreams that telepathy, if it influences our dreams, would be most likely to manifest itself in deep sleep.

Bergson ended his lecture on a hopeful note. He hoped that through the study of the unconscious, to which the best approach is dreams, we might one day resolve the enigmas that still perplex us. His quest led him to accept the presidency of the British Society for Psychical Research (1913) and to study at first hand the case of Eusapia Palladino (1854-1918), the Italian medium who, though she showed but little understanding of the feats which she was able to perform in both light and dark—levitation of furniture and apparitions of the dead —baffled the scientific world for a period of twenty years.

Much mystery still surrounds the subject of dreams. An understanding of their significance would be of great worth in psychoanalysis and in the treatment of mental patients; it would also contribute much toward the understanding of the thought-processes of normal people. Bergson even expressed the hope that mankind might one day cross over the threshold of the mystery adumbrated in his theory of dreams and win its greatest battle over matter, the enemy of the movement of life, by achieving immortality.

WADE BASKIN

Southern State College

THE WORLD OF DREAMS

What, then, is a dream? I perceive objects, yet there is nothing. I see men. I think that I speak to them and hear them answer me, yet there is no one and I say nothing. Everything happens *as if* there were real things and real persons, but upon awakening I find that everything has vanished. How does this come about?

To begin with, is it really true that there is nothing in the dream? In other words, is there not some *perceptible matter* that we can see, hear, feel, etc. when we are asleep as well as when we are awake?

Close your eyes and consider carefully what occurs on the field of vision. Many people when questioned on this point will say that nothing happens and that they see nothing. That is because a certain amount of practice is required for proper self-observation. But let the same people take the first step toward making the necessary effort and gradually through attentiveness they will be able to single out many different things. At first generally, a dark background. Occasionally against the dark background, bright dots which come and go, rise and fall, slowly and sedately. More often, spots of a thousand colors, sometimes dull but at other times and with certain people of an extraordinary brilliance which reality could never match. These spots expand and contract, change their shape and colors, constantly displace one another. Sometimes the change is slow and gradual but sometimes it is a whirlwind of bewildering swiftness.

What is responsible for this whole phantasmagoria? Physiologists and psychologists have studied the changing medley of colors; to describe the phenomenon they have used such terms as ocular spectrum, color spots, and phosphenes; they have attributed it to slight modifications that occur at all times as a result of retinal circulation and to pressure exerted on the eyes by the closed lids, resulting in the mechanical excitation of the optic nerve. But the explanation of the phenomenon and the terms used to identify it are not of primary importance. Everyone is familiar with the phenomenon. The point that I wish to make here is that it constitutes the raw material, the *stuff* that we use in shaping our dreams.

Some thirty or forty years ago Alfred Maury, and at about the same time D'Hervey, noticed that when we are about to fall asleep, the color spots with their changing shapes consolidate, become fixed, take on precise outlines—the very outlines of the objects and persons that will appear in our dreams. But that observation is slightly suspect, for it was made by psychologists who were half-asleep. Recently an American psychologist, Professor Ladd of Yale, devised a more exact method; his method is hard to apply, however, for it requires special training. It consists in acquiring the habit of keeping the eyelids closed on awakening in the morning and retaining for a short while the dream which otherwise would soon vanish from the field of vision and also, doubtlessly, from memory. Then the figures and objects in the dream are seen to dissolve gradually into phosphenes, the color spots which the eyes actually perceive when the lids are closed. Suppose, for instance, that in your dream you were reading a newspaper. On awakening you might find that in reality the well-defined outlines were blurred and that there remained nothing more than a white spot with scattered black lines. Or again, suppose that in your dream you were out on the open sea. As far as you could see, there stretched an endless expanse of yellowish-gray waves with their crowns of white spume. You might find on awakening that everything had fused into a huge spot, half yellow and half gray, sprinkled with bright dots. The spot was there and the bright dots were there all along. This would mean that our perception really has at its disposal during sleep a sort of *visual dust*, and that this dust is the source of our dreams.

But is it the only source? Restricting ourselves for the moment to the sense of sight, we must join to these visual sensations that might be called internal those that continue to come to us from an external source. Our eyes can still distinguish light from darkness and to a certain extent different kinds of light even after the lids are closed.

The sensations of light that come from without are responsible for many of our dreams. The sudden lighting of a candle in his room will suggest to the sleeper, unless he is sleeping too soundly, a dream dominated by the image of fire. Allow me to quote two of Tissié's observations on this point:

Leon B—— dreamed that the theater in Alexandria was on fire; the flames lighted up the whole district. Suddenly he found himself transported to a fountain in the middle of a great forum. Fire spanned the chains linking the thick posts set up around the fountain. Then he found himself back in Paris at the exposition, which was on fire . . . ; he witnessed some heart-rending scenes, etc. He awoke with a start. On his eyes fell the rays from a dark lantern which the night nurse had flashed toward his bed in passing.

Bertrand M—— dreamed that he had enlisted in the marine infantry in which he had previously served. He went to Fort-de-France, Toulon, Lorient, the Crimea, and Constantinople. He saw lightning and heard thunder. . . . Finally he took part in a battle in which he saw fire leap from the mouths of cannon. He awoke with a start. Like B—— he had been awakened by a flash of light from the dark lantern turned on him by the night nurse.

Such are the dreams often caused by sudden exposure to bright light.

Quite different are the dreams suggested by soft, continuous light, like moonlight. A. Krauss relates that upon awakening one day he discovered that he was still extending his arms toward something which he saw in his dreams as the image of a girl. Slowly the image fused with that of the full moon, which was bathing him in its rays. Oddly enough, there are other examples of dreams in which moonlight, caressing a sleeper's eyes, gives rise to visions of maidens. This suggests a kindred origin for the classical fable of Endymion, the shepherd thrown into a deep sleep and caressed while sleeping by Selene, the goddess of the moon.

I have been discussing only visual sensations. They are the main ones. But auditive sensations also play an important part in our dreams.

First, our ears perceive internal sensations—humming, buzzing, whistling—which are hard to isolate and identify in the waking state but which are distinct in sleep. Next, we continue after falling asleep to hear external noises. A creaking piece of furniture, a crackling fire, the rain lashing a window, the wind playing a chromatic scale in the chimney—all these sounds reach our ears and are converted by dreams, according to circumstances, into conversation, songs, shouts, music, etc. Scissors were grated on tweezers near Alfred Maury's ears while he was asleep. Soon he dreamed that he was hearing the tocsin and witnessing the events of June, 1848. There are countless instances of similar observations and experiences. But I hasten to add that sounds do not play in our dreams so important a part as colors. Our dreams are by and large visual, and even more visual than we think. Most of us at one time or another—as Max Simon has observed—have dreamed about speaking to someone or being engaged in a lengthy conversation only to have forced upon us the singular realization that we were not speaking and had not spoken, and that our interlocutor had not uttered a single word. We had

exchanged our thoughts and carried on an un-
equivocal conversation, yet we had heard
nothing. This fact is easily explained. For us to
hear sounds in our dreams it is generally necessary for us to perceive real noises. We can not
start from scratch. Unless we are provided with
some phonic substance, it is hard for us to fabri-
cate sounds in our dreams.

Much more might be said about tactile sensations than about auditive sensations, but our
time is limited. We could speak for hours about
the singular phenomena that stem from the fact
that our sense of touch continues to function,
though indistinctly, during sleep. These sensations assail and characteristically modify or
reshape the images that occupy our field of
vision. Often in the dead of night we suddenly
sense the contact of our bodies with our light
clothing; this *reminds* us that we are lightly clad.
Then we expose ourselves, if we happen to be
dreaming about walking in the street, in our
modest garb to the eyes of passers-by—seem-
ingly without causing them to be astonished.
We are at times astonished in our dreams but
no one ever seems to be astonished by our
actions. I mention this dream because it is a

common one. Another dream which many of you must have had is this one: You feel that you are flying through the air or floating in space. If you have ever had such a dream, you can be almost certain that it will be repeated. Each time that it recurs, you will reason in this way: "Previously in dreams I have had the illusion of flying through the air or of floating in space, but this is the real thing. This proves to me conclusively that we can defy the law of gravitation." Now if you awaken suddenly from the dream, you will have no difficulty in analyzing it, provided that you lose no time in making the attempt. You will see that you were acutely aware of the fact that your feet were not on the ground. And still, since you did not believe that you were asleep, you had lost sight of the fact that you were lying down, with the result that in your dream you were not in bed and yet did not have your feet on the ground. You concluded quite naturally that you were floating in space. Notice that when levitation is accomplished by flight, only one side of your body makes an effort to fly. And if you awaken at that moment, you will find that the sensation of making an effort to fly coincides with the actual sensation produced by the pressure of your body against the bed. The sensation of pressure, dissociated from its cause, transformed into a sensation of effort pure and simple, and joined to the illusion of floating in space, may be sufficient to produce the dream.

It is interesting to observe how sensations of pressure, by moving up toward the field of vision and taking advantage of the luminous dust found there, manage to change into shapes and colors. Max Simon relates that he once had a strange, distressing dream. He dreamed that he had before him two unequal stacks of gold coins which for some reason he had to make equal. He could not succeed and was distressed by his failure. His anxiety, increasing in intensity as the dream progressed, finally awoke him. He then noticed that one of his legs was caught in the folds of the blanket in such a way that his feet were on different levels, making it impossible for him to align them. Hence the feeling of inequality which, invading the field of vision and finding there one or more yellow spots (this is at any rate the hypothesis that I offer), was expressed visually through the inequality of the two stacks of gold coins. Immanent in the sensations of touch experienced during sleep is the tendency to visualize ourselves and thereby to put ourselves into our dreams.

Even more important than tactile sensations proper are the sensations related to what has sometimes been called the internal senses. These deep-seated sensations emanate from every organ and especially from the viscera. One would hardly suspect that these internal sensations could become so acute during sleep. They are doubt-lessly present in the waking state but go un-noticed as a result of our being engaged in different activities. We live outside ourselves. But sleep brings us back inside ourselves. It frequently happens that people subject to laryn-gitis and tonsillitis dream that they are having a recurrence of their ailment and feel an un-pleasant tingling in their throats. Awake, they no longer feel anything and believe that the tingling was an illusion. But a few hours later the illusion becomes a reality.

Serious illnesses and accidents, epileptic at-tacks, cardiac diseases, etc. have in some instances been anticipated almost prophetically in dreams. We should not be surprised, therefore, to find that philosophers like Schopenhauer have seen in dreams a repercussion upon our consciousness of disturbances which emanate from the sympathetic nervous system, that psychologists like Scherner have attributed to each of our organs the power to provoke a definite class of dreams which in some way represent it symbolically, and finally, that doctors like Artigues have written treatises on the semiological value of dreams, *i.e.* the means of using dreams for diagnosing certain illnesses. More recently Tissié, mentioned earlier, has shown how specific dreams are related to affections of the digestive, respiratory, and circulatory systems.

Let me summarize. When we fall into a natural sleep we must not think, as some people sometimes imagine, that our senses are shut off from external impressions. Our senses continue to function. It is true that they function with less precision, but in return they embrace a host of subjective impressions which pass unnoticed in the waking state—when we live in a world of perceptions common to all men—and which reappear in sleep when we live only for ourselves. Our faculty of sensory perception, far from shrinking in every respect when we are asleep, broadens its field of operations. It is true that it often loses in energy and *tension* what it gains in *extension,* for it rarely brings us anything other than vague impressions. These impressions are the materials with which we build our dreams. But they are only the materials; by themselves they could never yield dreams.

They could never yield dreams by themselves because they are vague and indeterminate. I am speaking only of the impressions that play an important part in our dreams: the changing colors and shapes that evolve before our eyes as soon as the lids are closed. They never have well-defined outlines. Take black lines against a white background. To the dreamer they may stand for a page in a book, the front of a new house with dark shutters, or any number of other things. Who will make the choice? What shape will his decision imprint on the indecisive substance? The shape will depend on his remembrances.

Note that as a rule dreams create nothing. Artistic, literary or scientific productions have of course been attributed in some instances to dreams. I shall mention only the well-known anecdote told about Tartini, a violinist and composer of the past century. Finding the muse recalcitrant when he tried to compose a sonata, he fell asleep; in his dream he saw the devil, who wrested from him his violin and gave a masterful rendition of the elusive sonata. Tartini wrote it down from memory when he awoke. It has come down to us as "The Devil's Sonata."

But it is difficult in dealing with older cases to separate history from legend. We need first-hand observations of unquestionable authenticity. About the only one that I have been able to find is that of the contemporary English novelist Stevenson. In a striking essay entitled "A Chapter on Dreams" this author, who was endowed with rare analytical talent, explained how the most original of his novels were composed or at least sketched out in his dreams. But you will find on reading the chapter carefully that at a certain period in his life Stevenson had reached a psychological state in which it was difficult for him to tell whether he was asleep or awake. At least that is my interpretation of the facts.

When the mind creates—I mean when it is capable of exerting the organizing and synthe-sizing effort required for overcoming an obstacle or solving a problem and to an even greater degree for producing a viable work of the imagination—we are not actually asleep, or the part of us that is at work is not the same at any rate as the part that is asleep; we can not say, therefore, that the mind is dreaming. In true sleep—in sleep that involves our whole being— remembrances are first and foremost in the warp and woof of our dreams. But we often fail to recognize them. They may be very old remembrances of which we are oblivious during the waking state—remembrances drawn from the darkest depths of our past. They may be (and often are) memory images of which we are but vaguely, almost unconsciously aware during the waking state. Or again, they may be fragments of shattered remembrances which we have collected piecemeal and woven haphazardly into an unrecognizable and incoherent fabric.

Confronted with these odd collections of images with no plausible meaning, our intelligence (which, contrary to what some people have asserted, does not abdicate its power of reasoning during sleep) searches for an explanation, tries to fill in the gaps. It fills them by calling up other remembrances which, because they have the same deformations and the same inconsistencies as the former, evoke in their turn still other remembrances—and so on indefinitely. But I shall not dwell on this point at the moment. It is enough for me to say, in answer to the question asked earlier, that the force which puts to constructive use the materials made available to dreams by the different senses—the force which converts into specific, well-defined objects the vague, indeterminate sensations which we receive through our eyes and ears as well as from the whole surface and interior of our bodies —is memory.

Memory! In the waking state many remembrances come and go, occupying our minds by turns. But they are always linked closely to our present activity. Here I recall D'Hervey's book on dreams. That is because I am discussing the question of dreams here in the Institut Psychologique, because my presence in this place and the activity that I am called upon to perform —the lecture that I am giving—direct the functioning of my memory along a certain specific course. The remembrances that we evoke when we are awake, no matter how remote they may at first appear, are always linked in some way to our present activity.

What is the function of memory in an animal? It is to recall to the animal in a specific situation the helpful or harmful consequences that may have issued previously from similar situations and thereby to direct its course of action. Doubtlessly the memory of man, though not subservient to it in the same degree, is also linked to his present activity. Our remembrances at a given moment form a coherent whole—a pyramid, as it were, whose peak is wedged into our present activity.

Behind the remembrances associated with our employment and revealed through it, however, are others, thousands of others, stored away in the depths of the memory, down beneath the stage lighted by consciousness. Yes, I believe indeed that all our past life is there, preserved in its most intimate details, that we never forget anything, and that everything which we have felt, perceived, thought and willed since the first stirrings of our consciousness lives on indestructibly. But the remembrances preserved in the darkest depths are like invisible phantoms. Perhaps they are drawn toward the light but dissuaded from ever making the attempt to reach it by the knowledge that such an undertaking is hopeless and that I, a living, acting being, have to do something other than concern myself with them.

Now suppose that at a certain moment I become *disinterested* in the present situation or activity—in short, disinterested in everything that has been holding and directing my memory up to that moment. Suppose, in other words, that I fall asleep. Then, sensing that I have just removed the obstacle, lifted the trap door that has been keeping them in the substratum of my consciousness, the remembrances spring forth. They leap up, bestir themselves, perform a great dance of death in the night of the unconscious. And, all together, they rush toward the door that has just been opened slightly. They would all like to pass through it. They can not, however, for there are too many of them. From the multitude called, which ones will be chosen? The outcome is not hard to predict. Earlier, while I was awake, the remembrances that managed to break through were those related in some way to the present situation, to what I could see and hear around me. Now the images that crowd my field of vision are more vague, the sounds that strike my ears more turbid, the tactile sensations

that come to me from all over my body more
indistinct, but the sensations that issue from the
innermost parts of my system are more numer-
ous. Among the phantom remembrances that
aspire to fill themselves with color and sound—
with substance, in short—the only ones to
succeed will be those that can assimilate the
colors that we glimpse, the external and internal
noises that we hear, etc. and correspond in addition to the affective tone of our general sen-
sibility. When this union between memory and
sensation is effected, we have a dream.

In a poetic passage of his *Enneads*, the philosopher Plotinus, Plato's interpreter and successor,
explains how men come into being. Nature, he
says, roughs out living bodies. But she provides
nothing more than the skeletal form. Without
help from another source she could never complete her task. But souls dwell in the world of
ideas. Unable to act by themselves and not even
thinking of independent action, they float around
beyond time and space. Certain bodies, however,
correspond more closely than others by virtue
of their shape to the aspirations of certain souls.
And certain souls identify themselves with certain bodies. A body, not wholly viable when it

leaves the hand of nature, rises toward the soul
that will make its life complete. And the soul,
looking upon this body and believing that it sees
its image in the body as in a mirror, is attracted
and enthralled; it drops down, and its fall is life.
To these detached souls I would compare the
remembrances immersed in the darkness of the
unconscious. Our nocturnal sensations, on the
other hand, resemble incomplete bodies. Sensations are warm, colorful, lively and almost
alive, but indecisive. Remembrances are complete but airy and lifeless. Each sensation is
trying to find a form on which to mold its vague
outlines. Each remembrance is seeking to obtain
some substance to fill it, to provide it with ballast
—in short, to bring about its actualization. They
exert a mutual attraction and the phantom remembrance, incarnated in the sensation that
provides it with flesh and blood, becomes a being
with a life of its own—a dream.

There is nothing mysterious about the birth
of a dream. It resembles the birth of a perception.
The mechanism of dreams is the same in its broad
outlines as that of normal perception. What we
actually see when we perceive a real object, in
fact—the concrete matter of our perception—

is insignificant in contrast to what our memory introduces. When you read a book or look over a newspaper, do you believe that every printed letter actually reaches your consciousness? If that were true, more than a whole day might be required for going over the newspaper. The truth is that in each word or even in each phrase you see but a few letters or characteristic marks —just enough to enable you to guess the rest. You think that you see the rest, but actually this is a hallucination. A number of conclusive experiments leaves no room for doubt on this point. I shall mention only the experiments of Goldscheider and Müller. These investigators copied or printed certain formulas in common use—"Positively No Admission," "Preface to the Fourth Edition," etc.—but were careful to write the words incorrectly by changing some letters and, above all, by omitting others. The expressions were exhibited in a darkened room. The person who was to serve as the subject in the experiment did not know, of course, what had been written on the placard in front of him. Each placard was lighted electrically for a very short time—not long enough for the observer to be able actually to perceive every letter. The

researchers began by determining experimentally
the time necessary for viewing one letter of the
alphabet; then it was easy for them to make it
impossible for the subject to glimpse more than
eight or ten letters, for example, out of a total
of thirty or forty contained in each expression.
The subject generally read the expression in its
entirety without difficulty. But for our purposes
that is not the most instructive point in the
experiment.

The subject was asked in each instance about
the letters which he was sure of having seen.
These letters might actually have been written
on the placard, or they might have been missing,
either because they had been replaced by others
or because they had been omitted. Thus the subject might see clearly outlined in the bright light
a letter which did not exist if that letter seemed
by virtue of its context to belong in the expression. The characteristics that actually made an
impression on the subject's eyes were therefore
used only to guide his unconscious memory.
When the appropriate remembrance was discovered—when the memory reconstructed the
expression presented in a skeletal form by these
characteristics—it was brought to the fore. This

remembrance, and not the writing on the placard, was what the subject saw. Thus the experiments clearly show that ordinary reading is mainly guesswork, but not abstract guesswork. It is an externalization of remembrances which manage by taking advantage of piecemeal realizations to realize themselves completely.

Thus it is that in the waking state and in the cognizance that we take of concrete objects around us, there is in operation a process identical in nature to the process of dreaming. We perceive but the skeletal form of a thing; this rough outline summons the complete remembrance, which is either in the unconscious or simply in the state of thought; profiting by the occasion, the complete remembrance rushes out. It is this type of hallucination, packaged and framed in a concrete setting, that we perceive. This is much shorter and is accomplished more quickly than the thing itself. Interesting studies might also be made of the behavior and appearance of remembrances during the process. We must not assume that our remembrances are stored away as inert imprints. They are kept in our memory like steam in a boiler, more or less under *pressure*.

When the skeletal form that the viewer has

glimpsed sends out its summons, remembrances seem to come together in family groups according to their bonds of kinship and resemblance. Some of Münsterberg's experiments (earlier than those of Goldscheider and Müller), even though conducted for a different purpose, seem to me to confirm this hypothesis. Münsterberg wrote his words correctly. Nor did he use stereotyped expressions; he used isolated words chosen at random. In his experiments also, the words were exposed for such a short time that they could not be perceived in their entirety. While the subject was looking at one of the written words, another word with a completely different meaning was shouted in his ear. Examples: The word shown was *tumult*, the word shouted, *train;* the word given by the subject was *tunnel.* The word shown was *Triest,* the word shouted, the German word *Verzweiflung* (despair); the word recalled by the subject was *Trost* (comfort). Thus everything happened as if when pronounced close to the subject's ear, the word train had awakened, without his knowing it, hopes of conscious realization on the part of a host of remembrances related to the idea of train (car, rail, trip, etc.); but these were only hopes, and the memory image that actually appeared was the one that the sensation had already begun to realize.

Such is the mechanism of true perception and also of dreams. In each instance there are on the one hand concrete impressions made on the sense organs and on the other, remembrances that have come to be incorporated in the impressions and revived by their vitality.

But precisely what is the essential difference between perceiving and dreaming? What does it mean to sleep? Needless to say, I am not asking for a physiological explanation of sleep. That is a special issue and one that is in addition far from being resolved. I am asking for a psychological explanation of sleep. For our mind continues to function while we sleep; it functions, as we have just seen, with elements similar to those used during the waking state—with sensations and remembrances; and in much the same way it puts them together. Yet on the one hand we have normal perception and on the other, dreams. What, then, I repeat, is the difference between them? And what is the psychological basis of sleep?

Theories are to be regarded with distrust. And there are many theories of sleep. One theory is that sleeping consists in isolating ourselves from the external world, in closing our senses to things from the outside. But I have shown that our senses continue to function during sleep, that they provide us with the rough outlines or at least the starting point for most of our dreams. Falling asleep, according to some people, means stopping the functioning of the higher mental faculties. And they talk of some kind of temporary paralysis of the higher cerebral centers. I do not believe that this is much closer to the truth. In our dreams we of course become *indifferent* to logic, but we do not become *incapable* of exercising it. In some dreams we reason soundly and even subtly. I would almost say—at the risk of seeming paradoxical— that the dreamer's mistake is in reasoning too much. He would rule out folly if he acted merely as a spectator attending the parade staged by the images in his dreams. But he is certain to resort to whimsical reasoning bordering on foolishness when he makes every effort to explain what he sees, for then he must tie together incoherent images. I am of course aware of the fact that our higher intellectual faculties flag during sleep and that for the most part the dreamer's powers of reasoning are so weak as to seem at times like a parody of reasoning. But as much could be said of every other faculty during sleep. Dreams are therefore characterized neither by the abolition of reasoning nor by the closing of the senses. The answer must be sought elsewhere.

Something more than theories is required. We must come directly into contact with the facts. Researchers must use themselves as subjects in conclusive experiments. On coming out of a dream—for he can hardly analyze himself while the dream is in progress—the subject should watch for the transition between sleeping and waking, clinging as tightly as possible to the transition, and then force himself to express in words all that he has experienced during the transition. That is very difficult, but it can be accomplished through attentiveness. Allow me to borrow from my own experience and relate both a recent dream and what was accomplished on coming out of the dream.

I dreamed that I was addressing an audience, making a political speech at a political rally. And from the back of the auditorium there came a murmur. The murmur grew louder, like a rumble. Then it became a roar, a frightful tumult. And finally there resounded throughout the auditorium the rhythmic shout: "Throw him out! Throw him out!" At that instant I awoke. A dog was barking in a near-by garden, and each *wow-wow* blended with a shout: "Throw him out!" So there was the infinitesimal moment that must be grasped. My waking self, which had just reappeared, had to turn around toward the self in my dreams, which was still there, and for a few instants at least hold on to it, keep it from getting away.

"I have caught you in the act. You thought that you heard an audience shouting, but it was only a dog barking. You are going to tell me what you were doing!"

To that the self in my dream replied: "*I wasn't doing anything*, and that is precisely how you and I differ from one another. You suppose that you don't have to do anything at all to hear a dog bark and know that it is a dog barking. That is a big mistake. Without realizing it, you put forth a considerable effort.

"This is what you do. You take your whole

memory, all your cumulative experience, and you cause this formidable mass of remembrances to converge on a single point in such a way as to inject into the sound that you actually hear the most appropriate sound that can be drawn from all your remembrances. And you achieve a perfect correspondence; there must not be the slightest discrepancy between the remembrance that you call up and the crude sensation that you receive (otherwise you would still be dreaming); you can achieve this perfect correspondence only through an effort of both your memory and your perception, just as the tailor when fitting you for a suit stretches the pieces of cloth and adjusts them to the shape of your body in order to pin them. So you see, at every moment during the day, you are putting forth an enormous effort. Your waking life is a life of toil even when you think that you are doing nothing, for at every instant you must choose and at every instant exclude. You choose—and with extreme precision and subtlety—between remembrances, rejecting any remembrance which will not fit in exactly with your present state. The choice that you are forever exercising, the adaptation that you are forever in the process of making, is the first and most important attribute of what is called good sense. But all this keeps you in a state of uninterrupted *tension*. You don't feel it at this very moment any more than you feel atmospheric pressure, but in the long run you become tired. Good sense is tiresome.

"Well, I repeat, I differ from you for the very reason that I do nothing. I simply refuse to make the effort that you are forever making. Instead of becoming attached to life, I become detached from it. I become indifferent to everything. Sleeping means becoming disinterested. You sleep in proportion to your disinterest. A mother sleeping beside her child may not stir at the sound of thunder, yet awaken at the whimper of the child. She is not really asleep with respect to the child. We do not sleep with respect to what continues to interest us.

"You ask me what I do when I dream. I'll tell you what you do when you are awake. You take me, your dreaming self, me, the totality of your past, and you manage by making me smaller and smaller to fit me into the tiny circle which you draw around your present activity. That is what it means to be awake and to live a psychologically normal life. It means struggling. It means willing. As for dreams, do you really need an explanation? It is the state into which you naturally fall back as soon as you give yourself up, as soon as you no longer have the strength to concentrate on a single point, as soon as you stop *willing*. Something more likely to call for an explanation is the wonderful mechanism through which your will instantaneously and almost unconsciously manages at a particular moment to concentrate everything that you are carrying around inside yourself on one and the same point, the point that interests you. But to explain that is the task of normal psychology, the psychology of the waking state, for *waking* and *willing* are one and the same."

That is what my dreaming self might have said. And it might tell us many other things if we could let it speak freely. But I see that our time has already elapsed. Let us hastily extract from this lecture the basic difference between dreaming and the waking state. The same faculties function when we dream and when we are awake, but in one instance they are tense and in the other relaxed. The fullness of our mental life is in our dreams, but with a minimum of tension, effort, and bodily movement. We still perceive, still remember, still reason; all this may abound in dreams, for in the domain of the mind, abundance does not mean effort. What requires effort is *precision of correspondence*. No effort is required for the sound of a barking dog to evoke the remembrance of a murmuring, shouting audience. But a positive effort is required for this sound to be perceived as the barking of a dog. The dreamer does not have the ability to make this effort. That is the one and only difference between him and a man who is awake.

From this basic difference many others could be deduced. The main characteristics of dreams would be readily understood. But here I can only outline the form which an extensive study of dreams should take. It would be carried out along three main lines: the incoherence of dreams, the abolition of the sense of duration which often appears to characterize dreams, and the *order* in which remembrances present themselves to the dreamer to contend for the waiting sensations in which they will be incorporated.

The incoherence of dreams seems to me to be easily explained. Since a dream characteristically exhibits, not a perfect correspondence but rather some variance between memory and sensation, quite different remembrances may be suited to the same sensation. Suppose, for instance, that in the field of vision there is a green spot with white dots. It may be a lawn spotted with white flowers, a billiard-table and billiard-balls, or a host of other things. These different remembrances, all capable of profiting by the same sensation, rush toward it. Sometimes all the remembrances cluster around a sensation at the same time, and then the lawn actually is a billiard-table. This accounts for the absurd dreams in which an object retains its identity while becoming something else. As I said a moment ago, the mind when confronted with such preposterous sights seeks an explanation and often, in so doing, simply adds to the incoherence.

As for the abolition of the sense of time in many of our dreams, this is another effect stemming from the same cause. A dream can offer us in a few seconds a series of events which during the waking state would occupy whole days. You are acquainted with the case mentioned by Maury; it has become a classic, and I accept it as probable in spite of recent adverse criticism because of the great number of similar

observations that I have found scattered throughout the literature of dreams. But there is no
mystery about the precipitation of images. In
the waking state we live our lives in common
with our fellow beings; attentiveness to this
external, social bond holds sway over the suc-
cession of our internal states. It is like the
pendulum which lessens and cuts up into regular
segments the undivided, almost instantaneous
tension of the mainspring in a clock. It is the
pendulum that is missing in dreams. Precipitation
is not any more so than abundance a sign of effort
in the domain of the mind. Precision of correspondence, I repeat, is what requires effort. And
that is precisely what the dreamer lacks. He is no
longer capable of the *attentiveness to life* necessary for regulating the inner according to the
outer, for fitting inner duration perfectly into
the general duration of things.

Finally, there remains the question of how the
peculiar relaxation of the mind during dreams
explains the preference shown by the dreamer
for one remembrance over another one equally
capable of being incorporated in actual sensations. According to one current theory, we
dream mainly about events that have especially

preoccupied us during the day. That is sometimes true, but when the psychological life of
the waking state is carried over in that way into
our sleep, the result is that we hardly sleep. Sleep
filled with such dreams would leave us exhausted.
In normal sleep our dreams relate rather, all other
conditions being equal, to the thoughts that have
flashed by us like lightning or to objects that we
have perceived almost without awareness. If we
dream of events of the same day, the most insignificant facts, not the most important ones,
will have the best chance of reappearing.

Here I am in complete agreement with W.
Robert, Delage, and Freud. I was in the street,
waiting for a streetcar. I was waiting beside the
tracks and was not in the slightest danger. Nevertheless, if the idea of possible danger had crossed
my mind just as the streetcar came by—how
shall I put it?—if my body had instinctively re-
coiled even though I was not conscious of feeling
any fear, that night I might have dreamed that
the streetcar was running over me. I was watch-
ing over a patient whose condition was hopeless.
If I had once chanced to hope against all hope
without being aware of it, I might have dreamed
that the patient had recovered. I would be more

likely in any case to dream of recovery than
of sickness. In short, the events that are most
likely to reappear in dreams are those to which
we are least attentive in our thinking. What is
unusual about that? A dreaming self is a relaxed
self. It welcomes most readily incidental, dis-
tracting remembrances not characterized by
effort.

It may be true that in very deep sleep the laws
governing the reappearance of remembrances are
quite different. We know almost nothing about
deep sleep. The dreams that fill it are as a general
rule dreams that we forget. Sometimes, however,
we recall some part of them. And then we experience a strange, untranslatable feeling. It
seems that we are returning from afar—from
far away in space and time. These are doubt-
lessly very old scenes from our youth or childhood which in our dreams we revive in all their
details, changed somewhat by the emotional
coloring that we have added but impregnated
with a youthful, childlike freshness that we
might seek in vain to re-create during the waking
state. I believe that some recent unpublished
experiments by Vaschide will throw some light
on deep sleep and show that these dreams are

more coherent than the ones which we ordinarily remember.

It is toward deep sleep that psychologists should direct their efforts in order not only to study the mechanism of the unconscious memory but also to examine the more mysterious phenomena relating to "psychical research." I dare not make any pronouncements on these phenomena, but I can not refrain from attaching some importance to the data collected systematically and with tireless zeal by the Society for Psychical Research which we were told about the other day. If telepathy influences our dreams, it probably has the best opportunity to manifest itself during very deep sleep. But, I repeat, I can make no pronouncement on this point. I have gone forward with you as far as possible. I stop at the threshold of the mystery. To explore the innermost depths of the unconscious, to work in what I have called earlier the substratum of consciousness, that will be the main task of psychology in the century that is dawning. I do not doubt that wonderful discoveries await it there, as important perhaps as were in the preceding centuries the discoveries in the physical and natural sciences. That, at any rate, is the promise that I make, the wish that I express in closing. And to you, ladies and gentlemen, I am grateful for the constant attentiveness with which you have followed this address from the beginning to the end, even though it has exceeded by far the prescribed length.

CPSIA information can be obtained
at www.ICGtesting.com
Printed in the USA
LVOW12s1034040916
503165LV00001B/47/P